Cross the Divide

CW00739341

Roger Carr

HORWITZ
MARTIN
EDUCATION

HORWITZ
MARTIN
EDUCATION

Horwitz Martin Education
A Division of Horwitz Publications Pty Ltd
55 Chandos St
St Leonards NSW 2065
Australia

Horwitz Martin Education
Unit 15, Cressex Enterprise Centre
Lincoln Road
High Wycombe, Bucks HP12 3RL
United Kingdom

a black dog book
Designed by Josie Semmler
Illustrations by Rachel Tonkin pp. 2, 3, 10, 16, 21, 27, 31, 44, 48, 52, 56, 63,
73, 81, 87.
Cover illustration by Mini Goss
Printed and bound in Australia by Hyde Park Press.

National Library of Australia
Cataloguing information
Carr, Roger Vaughan, 1937–.
  Crossing the divide.

Bibliography
ISBN 0 7253 1952 6.

I. Title. (Series: Phenomena II).

A823.3

Thoth
The Egyptian
god of wisdom,
mathematics and writing.

1 2 3 4
00 01 02

Contents

Family Tree

Abel Covey (born 1840–died 1889)	*married*	**Amelia Kilroy** (born 1843–died 1920)

Children

*William
(born 1864–died 1934)
Sarah
(born 1866–died 1943)

*William Covey	*married*	**Rita Mandeville** (born 1873–died 1930)

Children

Gaye (born 1894–died 1982)	**Frederick** (born 1900–died 1962)
*Thomas (born 1896–died 1980)	**Herbet** (born 1907–died 1987)
Dorothy (born 1898–died 1975)	

*Thomas Covey	*married*	**Adrienne Hatton** (born 1900–died 1990)

Children

*William
(born 1923–)
Doreen
(born 1926–died 1999)

*William Covey	*married*	**Virginia Vaughan** (born 1926–died 1988)

Child

*Margot
(born 1961–)

*Margot (Mum)	*married*	**David Longford** (Dad) (born 1963–)

Child

Abi
(born 1988–)

chapter 1

Abi's e-book

ABI STOPPED to gaze across the roofs of the city toward the distant mountains. They rose, hazy blue in the afternoon light and she closed her eyes a moment to dream. But it was a moment too long. When she opened them again the bus was already gone.

"Oh!" she cried. But she didn't really mind. She had plenty of time.

It was a warm day and she sat on the edge of the grass to wait. She often wondered if the wagon train had come this way.

Abi smiled, her mind returning to the journal Abe Covey, her great-great-great-grandfather had kept. Mum and Dad had put a copy of the original journal onto an e-book reader and given it to her for her birthday. She took it everywhere with her.

1

She pulled it from her bag, and keyed in a search for mountains...

My horse moved at a slow walk, keeping pace with the wagon that Amelia drove. The four oxen plodded mindlessly on, their eyes showing no interest. Their heads were down, lifting only when Amelia cracked the whip to remind them to keep moving.

In the far distance were the mountains which had caught my fancy, and I said to my Milly what a beautiful sight they were.

She just smiled at me from the seat of the wagon. She said it was about the ten-thousandth time I had said that same thing, and called me a dreamer whose mind was always on the other end of the rainbow.

Maybe she's right. I've always had an urge to see what lies beyond any horizon.

I reached out a hand to touch hers as the wagon jolted across the rough tussocks of grass that made up the plain here. Then my eyes moved back to the silhouette of the mountain range ahead, still three or four weeks ride away.

We had first seen them a month or more ago. Then they were just a smudge on the western horizon—but smudge enough for me to make a promise to myself that one day

I would venture beyond them, just to see what was on the other side. I've always been that way, and Amelia has accepted that it's the way I'll always be.

Seven months ago we had married, and that same day left the valley where we had grown up. She drove the new wagon I had mostly built myself. I drove the two hundred cattle that were to become the beginning of our new life. Our honeymoon had been the six-week trek to meet up with the wagon train going west.

While we were crossing the turkey plain today, our party came close to tragedy. The wagon that travels directly ahead of us carries Catherine Downward and her three young children. Mrs Downward must have become distracted, for she drove her wagon out of the wheel-lines of those ahead. The front left wheel went into a water-wash, and the wagon went half over, pitching the youngest child quite high into the air.

Abi smiled. She liked this part of the journal. She checked her watch. The next bus was not due for another few minutes. She closed her eyes for a few moments to imagine the scene, then returned to reading the journal…

Of fortune, I was taking my rest from the cattle, riding alongside my Amelia to chat. When I saw the wagon begin to fall I put spurs to my horse, and was as much surprised as the child, Marion, when I reached her in time to actually take her from the air in one arm.

She was unharmed, but the wagon rolled right over on its side, and required a day of work to repair.

We called ahead to camp, then I went forward and had a good hard talk to Joe Feather, our guide. He should have marked such a water-wash with a stake. That's his job. He became ill-tempered with my criticism, and took his things and left us forthwith…

Abe Covey would have written his journal with a pen dipped in ink.

Abi stood and walked across to the bus stop. Even then she was still thinking of the journal. It had been written between 1860 and 1889. The original journal took up five huge books. It had been written on single sheets of paper, then bound into volumes. Abi's parents had taken it to be scanned and put onto a CD. Then they had duplicated the CD and sent copies to the other descendants of Abe Covey so there would always be a record, even if the original journals were lost in a fire or other accident.

For Abi, being given a copy on an e-book reader had been the best present she had ever received.

She looked again to the mountains. They were beautiful, and one day—she had promised herself for a long time now—she would set out on an adventure to the top of those mountains. She would go, as Abe Covey had promised himself, just to see what was on the other side.

One day soon, she said to herself as she climbed onto the bus. She was twelve, now. That was old enough.

It was Wednesday, and when Abi got home she took the basket of Grandad's freshly washed clothes and put it in the car port.

On Wednesdays they always went to the farm for the evening to see how Grandad was. They didn't really need to go. Lots of their family lived on the farms at the base of the mountains; and Abi's family spent most weekends there, too.

But it was only an hour's drive on the freeway, and a good excuse to breathe the fresh country air.

Abi filled the kettle and got the three

coffee mugs ready. She was impatient to be off, and the more she had ready when her parents, Dave and Margot, arrived home from work the more quickly they would get away. Then she switched on the television, and was still watching it when her mother came home.

"I'll start the kettle," Abi said.

"Dad already has." Her mother went on into the passage.

"Then I'll pack the car," Abi called.

She waved to her father as she ran through the kitchen. Then it was only the time needed for a drink and a quick change of clothes before they were away.

Lassoing is not just a cowboy's skill. Along with whip-cracking, it is now practised at competition level.

chapter 2

Grandad's farm

THE FREEWAY ran to the west from the city. Abi leaned forward from the back seat, as eager as ever to catch sight of the mountains. She smiled as they appeared ahead, sharply silhouetted by the setting sun that tinted their outline gold.

"I've just got to see what's on the other side!" Abi said, realising that both her parents had said exactly the same thing at the same time. They all laughed.

"You live in that journal, don't you!" her father said.

Abi grinned at his reflection in the rear-view mirror, then let her eyes return to the mountains. Perhaps it was about here that the Downward's wagon had gone over, and Abe had plucked the girl from the air.

She keyed in a search for Downward in her e-book…

…the Downward's wagon was back on its wheels halfway through the next day. We carried many spares among the sixteen wagons in the train, and there was little we could not replace or make new from wood along the trail.

Joe Feather had not returned by the time we started forward; but we knew the general direction, and that in a day or so Joe and his packhorses would suddenly appear ahead of us. He was a moody man, easily offended. The first time he had gone off after some minor argument we thought we would have to hold the train until we could find another guide. Then someone had discovered him a mile or so up the trail waiting for us.

It was just Joe Feather's way of showing his independence.

An hour or so after the wagons were rolling again, I left the cattle and rode back. I hitched my horse to the tailboard of the wagon and climbed aboard. I made up a lunch of broken bread and hunk meat for myself, and a prettier lunch for Amelia. We ate it together while she drove.

We had milking cows among the cattle, so

there was butter and milk for her; but I preferred the sweet stream water I had taken from the watercourse we had crossed a day or two back…

"I'm pleased they left the stream when they made the road," Dave said as the freeway swept over the valley.

"I wonder is it the same stream Abe Covey got the sweet water from?" Margot said.

"I'm sure it is," Abi said. "I always feel goose bumps when we cross it."

"You feel goose bumps just about everywhere from home to the farm," her mother laughed. "I think Abe Covey lives inside you."

"It feels like it, sometimes," Abi said. "That's why I have to finish the journey he began."

"Don't let's begin that argument again," Margot said.

"Grandad has been as far as Abe Covey went lots of times!" Abi shouted.

"Two or three times, at the most," Margot answered. "And anyway, he's always said what Abe Covey tried was too dangerous."

"Well I'm not going to take dangerous

Butter is made from cream. The cream is separated from the whole milk, then churned (stirred around) until part of it becomes semi-solid (the butter), and the remaining liquid (butter-milk) is drained off.

risks when I do it!" Abi said sulkily. "And I am going to do it, whatever you say!"

"When you're older—" Dave began.

"But I'm twelve, now!" Abi protested.

"Abi! No!" Margot snapped. "You're still far too young."

"I'm not!" Abi shouted.

"Abi! Not another word!"

Abi turned back to the journal…

It was a bad business last evening when the cattle were feeding out along a cottonwood stream. We only had one man, Slim Maloney, with them, as they were tired from the day's journey and content to graze and water on the green stream flats.

Slim says he was about asleep in the saddle himself when there was a commotion among the stock down in the cottonwoods.

He wasn't too worried, thinking perhaps a pair of young bulls were scoring off each other; testing themselves as young bulls will. He said he rode on down without hurry, and it was only when he came in sight of the creek itself that he knew what happened.

Twenty or thirty of the cattle had formed themselves in a rough circle, pawing at the ground and bellowing some. Slim said it was enough to cause him to unholster his rifle as

he rode down; which gave him time for the one shot he needed.

A young calf, with its throat torn out, was on the ground, with a cougar or mountain lion atop it.

Slim brought the lion's body back to the camp, and some of us went on back to the stream, but found no others.

Joe Feather says they mostly move about alone, so he thinks there's little chance of another being here.

It's a fine-looking animal, a light tawny brown. We reckon its tail at over two feet long, and the body, three or four. This one would have stood over two feet tall at the shoulder, and hefted, weighed maybe a hundred pounds.

Not fully grown, Joe Feather says.

We had a meeting about it later, and have decided none of the smaller children are to leave the sight of the wagons from now on.

I don't think these beasts would attack a man; but we think a child could be in mortal danger from them.

Grandad stirred the pot of Irish stew on the old wood stove, then tasted it. "Mmm, little weak on the tongue," he said to himself.

He added salt. "Ah, that's better," he said when he tasted it again.

The telephone rang and Grandad looked suddenly disappointed. "Don't tell me they can't come," he said to himself. He walked into the other room and picked up the phone.

"Hello?"

"Bill! It's Angus." Angus was Grandad's cousin, and lived on the next farm along. When Abe and Amelia Covey had settled, they had taken up land along the foot of the mountains. Over the years that land had been divided up among the children. Now there were five farms in a row owned by Abe and Amelia's descendants.

"You're sounding a little out of breath there, Angus," Grandad said into the telephone.

"Think you would be, too," Angus said. "I just had a run-in with a mountain lion."

"Ain't seen one of them in I don't know how long," Grandad said.

"Me neither," Angus said. "Just about forgot there were such critters. He got that young colt I told you about. The one that was born last week."

The mountain lion is also called panther, puma, painter, or catamount (which comes from cat-of-the-mountain).

"What!" Grandad said in surprise. "That's a shame, Angus."

"The mare was down on the cottonwood stream. Good place for shelter," Angus said. "I'd just ridden down to keep an eye on them. The mare was acting strange, then I saw the lion feasting on the colt. I had no gun, so I just stripped off the stirrup leather and rode down swinging that. Spooked the lion, all right. But that won't bring back the colt."

"What're you going to do?" Grandad asked. "I can come over with the dogs and a gun tomorrow and help with a hunt."

"No need," Angus said. "The park rangers are coming out tomorrow. I'd say they'll get it easy enough. I called to warn you. That lion went on down your way."

"I've got nothing very young around right now," Grandad said. "Don't think I've got much to interest it."

"But this is an old one with a bad leg," Angus said. "Limping when it ran off. park rangers say it's probably too hurt to run down a deer, so it'll try anything for a feed. They say they'll have to put it

The prey of the mountain lion includes mice, adult deer, wild pigs, rabbits and, in California, they have been known on occasions to attack joggers!

colt: *a young, male horse.*

down—it's even more dangerous now it's made one attack. They said I should warn everybody around this way."

"That sounds reasonable," Grandad agreed. "I'll keep a watch out."

"I'll let you know when they get it," Angus said.

Grandad put down the phone and went back into the kitchen. He was thoughtful as he stirred the stew, then turned his head quickly to listen as the dogs began to bark.

"Phew," he said, when he recognised their barking as friendly. He checked the old clock on the mantelpiece. "That'll be the folks."

Grandad took the plates from the warming oven, and began to fill them with the ladle. He was on the third plate before he began to puzzle. Usually a door would have slammed by now, and Abi would have rushed in like a small tornado. Was something the matter?

He was about to go and check when he heard car doors slam. His daughter, Margot, and her husband, Dave, came in.

"Hi, Grandad," Dave said. He'd got into the habit of calling his father-in-law by the same name Abi used for him.

A tornado can travel at speeds of over one hundred kilometres (sixty miles) per hour, destroying everything it touches.

14

"Hello, Dad," Margot kissed him before she carried the clean clothes through the inner door. "I'll just put these in your room."

"Thanks, lass," Grandad said, and frowned toward his son-in-law. "Something wrong, Dave? Where's Abi?"

"She started going on about the journey again," Dave said. "It got a little tense on the trip. She'll be in soon."

"Like Joe Feather," Grandad said as he went back to ladling the stew. "She sure is fixed on that dream."

"Too fixed," Margot said. She took the full plates to the table. "Twelve is just too young to set out on a journey like that."

"I've been doing some thinking on the matter, lass," Grandad said, pulling his chair up to the table. "I've been thinking—" He stopped as Abi came in, her face looking like a thunderstorm.

"Hi, Grandad," she mumbled as she came to the table.

"Good evening, Abi," Grandad said. "You going to spark some lightning at someone?"

"It's—" Abi began, but her mother cut her short.

"Not a word!" Margot snapped. "Not

one word or you can go to the car right
now and wait till we're ready to leave!"

Abi shot her mother a look that she
hoped would silence her, and shovelled
her food in. She hoped one of them
would tell her not to eat like that so she
could get into another argument. But they
all ignored her, knowing why she was
behaving so badly. As soon as she had
finished she said, "Can I leave the table?"
But she left before anyone answered.

She collected a handful of dog cubes
from the bag in the barn, fed some to the
dogs, then ran out to the fence of the
house-meadow. It was night, now, but,
when she called, Brittle whinnied from
down near the cottonwood trees by the
stream, and came at a gallop. He was
only four years old, and still had the
bursting energy of a quarter-horse colt.

Abi climbed through the fence and
hugged him, then fed him the dog cubes.

"They're all really stupid!" she said.
"You and I could get there by ourselves,
couldn't we?"

She pulled herself up onto his back and
lay down with her face in his mane.

"If Abe Covey was my father," she told
the horse, "he'd let us go by ourselves.

People in those days weren't frightened of anything."

Abi didn't notice the sudden, strange behaviour of the two dogs—the way they dropped their tails, and slunk back toward the house.

In the kitchen they finished clearing up, and pulled their chairs around the stove. Grandad added more wood, and new flames licked up from the disturbed ashes and began to crackle. The clock on the mantelpiece ticked loudly. Somewhere off in the night a cow bellowed mournfully.

"Had a call from cousin Angus just before," Grandad said. "A mountain lion killed one of his young colts today— down on the cottonwood stream."

"Did he shoot it?" Dave asked.

"Didn't have a gun. The park rangers are coming out to hunt it tomorrow."

Margot was suddenly concerned. "What about our horses?"

Grandad nodded. "I've been wondering about that, too. Angus said this lion was lame. That makes him more desperate—more dangerous."

Margot stood up. "Where's Abi?"

chapter 3

Panic in
the night

"**Y**OU DON'T THINK...?" Dave said to Grandad. But he didn't finish. Both men jumped up.

"Get a light," Grandad said. He took the bunch of keys from his pocket, and opened the gun safe. He lifted out a carbine, and dropped half-a-dozen shells into his pocket.

"She's not in the house!" Margot said, running through the kitchen and going out the back door.

Dad hitched the battery of the spotlight to his belt, and followed with Grandad.

"Abi!" Margot cried.

"What are you whining about!" Grandad shouted at the dogs. "Get 'em!"

---

carbine: *a light semi-automatic, or fully automatic rifle.*

But the dogs kept their tails down, and crept in close to his legs.

"There's something around," Dave said.

"Abi!" Margot cried again.

"What?" Abi's voice came. They hurried in the direction of Abi's voice and found her just inside the fence. She was still lying along Brittle's back. "I'm not doing anything!" she snapped.

"There's a rogue lion," Grandad said. "We're going to get the horses into the corral for the night."

Abi sat up. "I'll get them!"

"No. We'll all go," Grandad said. He called the dogs, but they wouldn't come.

"I've never seen them refuse before," Margot said, a slight shake in her voice.

"Nope," Grandad said. "They never have before."

Mum rested a hand on Brittle's mane, and they walked together across the field toward the cottonwood stream. The starlight was enough for them to see their way over the grassland, but the shapes of the cattle were indistinct.

"What about the cattle, Grandad?" Margot asked as they walked.

"Have to take their chance," Grandad

said. "Should be safe enough. No very young calves among them. And I don't think an old lion would tackle a full-grown beast out in the open. Horses concern me, though, with their habit of camping under the trees. Be tempting for a hungry animal to just drop down on one."

They squinted as they approached the deep black shadows of the cottonwoods. But they still couldn't see the horses.

"Give them a call," Grandad said as they approached the stream.

"Come on! Come on! Come on!" Margot called softly.

A horse nickered in response.

"I'll ride down—" Abi began, just as one of the horses screamed, and they heard it crash to the ground.

That bolted the other horses, and as they thundered past Abi kicked Brittle away and gave chase.

"Abi!" Margot screamed.

Grandad jacked a shell into the carbine, and fired into the air, the sound like a thunderclap, its echoes rolling back from the mountains.

At the same moment, Dave snapped on the spotlight and swept the cottonwoods with the bright white beam.

"Lion!" Margot screamed.

For one brief moment the blazing eyes of a big cat flashed back in reflection; then the lion swirled from the fallen body of the horse and was away through the cottonwoods.

"Get him!" Dave shouted, swinging the light to follow the big cat.

"The horse!" Grandad shouted.

Dave swung the beam back, just in time to see the terrified horse wrench to its feet and burst toward them in a mad panic.

Dave snapped off the light, and the three of them leapt from the path of the fear-crazed animal. It went like a black phantom across the grasslands in a rolling thunder of hooves.

"Abi!" Margot cried.

"She'll be all right, girl," Grandad said. "Worst that could happen now is she'll take a fall."

"Do you think we should we go after the lion?" Dave asked.

Grandad turned back up the paddock. "Nope," he said. "Just get them horses away safe. Leave the lion to the rangers."

But, as they hurried back toward the buildings, they were stopped by the sight of a bunch of horses swinging in a wild

gallop along the far side of the field. The sound of their pounding hooves came rolling back in echoes from the dark mountains.

"Look at that!" Grandad shouted. "Abi's still astride!"

"She hasn't even got a bridle on him!" Margot cried.

"That girl could ride the wind without a bridle!" Grandad said proudly.

Abi leaned forward, urging Brittle to the front of the bunch, then easing him across them.

"Steady…steady…easy!" she cried to calm them.

The frightened horses swung across the field, their pace easing at the sound of Abi's voice. Abi kept Brittle turning them—turning them until they became confused by their own circling, and calmed down to a trot. Then she rode out ahead and led them up toward the buildings. By the time the others had returned, she had all six horses in the home corral.

"Don't you ever do that again!" Margot cried as they reached her.

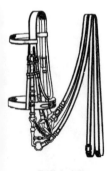

Full bridle for a horse.

"I didn't do anything!" Abi replied, offended. "I just got the horses!"

"Sorry," Margot said. "I'm…I'm just a little shaken."

The horses were still unsettled—snorting and pawing as they moved around the corral.

"We'll leave them in here for the night," Grandad said. "Not that I expect that lion back."

A horse can lose at least 5 litres (1.5 gallons) of blood before its health is in danger.

It only took a moment with the light to see it had been Logie Girl, one of Margot's horses, which had been attacked. There were three deep gashes on her back and blood on her neck where she had been bitten.

Margot wrapped her arms around Logie Girl's neck, and began to cry.

"Looks worse than it is," Grandad said, comforting Margot. "It's just scratches to a horse. I'll have the vet out and when you get back on Friday night they'll be well on their way to healing."

They drove home in silence. They had always known there were lions in the mountains. Abe Covey had mentioned them in his journal, and they themselves had sometimes seen partly eaten deer in the foothills. But, somehow, none of them had ever thought of a lion coming onto the farmland. It was scary and, even though she was tired from the visit, Abi couldn't sleep.

She reached for her e-book. She tapped "Kilroy" into the search box. Abi loved reading the bits about Mr Kilroy and Joe Feather

Old Jim Kilroy, a grizzled bear of a man, led the train while Joe Feather was away. I rode up beside him when lunch was done. Mister Kilroy knows a lot about the country—not this particular part, which is why we had hired Joe—but enough. I question him whenever I can.

I asked him did he think we would have any trouble crossing the mountains. But he said he didn't think we should even try to cross them. He said he had talked a lot with Joe Feather about them, and Joe said they were too steep and too broken for wagons. Maybe even too steep for driven cattle.

I explained to Mister Kilroy it was the other side of the mountains I wanted to see. The best cattle country of all might be beyond them. But Kilroy said it might be desert, too. To his mind it was best that we pushed on toward the grass Joe Feather promised was a few months journey ahead.

Mister Kilroy advised me to think of my Amelia and the family we would have.

When I protested, he just shook his head. When I asked him if he thought I was stubborn, I can still recall the exact words he used:

"Nothing wrong with being stubborn, son. Some people are always climbing mountains just to see what's on the other side. Stubborn people do some amazing things. But all I want is some good grass and some space I can fence out for my grandchildren."

Mister Kilroy shook his head. "But maybe it's because I'm old now. Maybe once I would have wanted to see what was on the other side, too."

We rode together, silent, for at least another hour. My eyes were on the mountains and my thoughts were on what was beyond. I guess Jim Kilroy's thoughts were on the grasslands Joe Feather had promised him.

Soon it was my turn to ride behind the cattle. As I turned my horse back, Mister Kilroy called out to me not to lose my dream.

I thanked him for those words.

Often, when mountain climbers are asked why they risk climbing difficult, dangerous mountains they reply, "Because it's there!"

chapter 4
Grandad's good idea

B ACK AT THE FARM for the weekend,
Grandad, Margot and Abi spent
Saturday cutting the nearly grown calves
from the mob to put them into a paddock
on their own. The calves didn't want to
leave their mothers, and the mothers
didn't want to leave their calves, so the
work was hard.

Grandad still rode, but he left the cutting
work to Margot and Abi. Dave stayed in
the house, doing the cashbooks, talking to
his buddies on the CB, and preparing the

meals. Even when he was a
boy, Dave had never really
been interested in cattle work.
He'd always wanted to ride
motorbikes, not horses. Abi
took after her mother rather
than her father in that respect.

A bull-calf with a white star turned
from the other calves and made a dash
for the mob. Abi spun Brittle around and
they took off after the calf. Abi leaned
and swung her short stockwhip just
ahead of the calf. The sudden crack of the
whip made him falter, and Brittle quickly
pushed in against him.

The calf bellowed, as it galloped back
toward the other calves. Its mother
answered. She tried to break out of the
main mob, but Margot already had Hit
Parade at a gallop, and turned her easily.

"Hurry them along, Abi!" Grandad
shouted.

There were fifty calves in the mob. Abi
kept them running hard enough to keep
their minds busy. It worked well, and
they were locked in before they knew it.

Abi swung to the ground and closed
the gate behind them. Then she mounted
Brittle again and let him burst away like a
drag racer. Dave said that quarter horses
were the first drag racers. They were bred
to run quarter-mile races—just like
today's drag cars. But a quarter horse
could stop without a parachute, and no
drag car could ever dodge and weave like
a quarter horse working cattle.

Abi eased Brittle to a walk between Grandad and Margot. They were putting the main mob in the back meadow, as far away from the calves as they could. They would need to be there for a week or so, to let the calves settle down and become used to living alone.

The back meadow was right against the start of the mountains, and Abi lifted her eyes to gaze at them. Their sides were dark in the evening light, and she wondered how they would look on their western side. The sun would still be shining on them there. Abi knew that one day she would see that.

Abe Covey had felt the same. Abi could remember the part where he said so.

She dug the e-book out of her saddlebag and keyed in a search for the dark side of the mountains…

Earlier this evening I was standing by the wagon and gazing at the dark side of the mountains that rose almost in front of us.

I remarked to Amelia that on the other side the sun would still be shining.

She replied that right where we were seemed fine to her. She liked the peace of this place below the mountains; and she was right when she said the grass was good. You could tell by the way the cattle enjoyed it.

Yet I still wondered if the grass might be even sweeter on the other side.

Amelia laughed at me when I said that. She was content for us to stay here, go on with the others, or to tackle the mountains on our own. She said it was up to me.

I told her I would go across to the meeting being held to plan the next stage, and that I would make up my mind then.

The wagons were spread out for the night on the grassy flats. Fires had been lit, and the scents of the evening meals cooking, and the woodsmoke, put a tang in the air.

The children from the wagons were playing. They enjoyed their freedom, now that their chores were done. But they were not alone. There was always one of us keeping watch on them—since that incident with the mountain lion.

The men were gathered in front of Jim Kilroy's wagon, and I made my way across the grass to where they talked. Joe Feather was squatting with them, drawing a map in a patch of bare earth.

I squatted to watch and listen.

Joe Feather pointed off to the side. That

was where the good grass was, he said. He drew a line on the map. A line that led away from the mountains.

I shook my head. I didn't plan to go that way at all. I wanted to go over the mountains. I argued that we should cross them, but none of the others agreed. Joe Feather said there was no pass that he knew of.

Then Gary Downward voted to go on to the good grass that Joe Feather said was ahead. Mister Kilroy voted with him.

That was enough. Everyone voted the same. Except me.

Mister Kilroy pointed out that it would be lonely for Amelia and I to stay behind. But my mind was made up…

"I'm going to stay," Abi said.

"Stay where?" Grandad asked in puzzlement.

Margot laughed. "Can't you see what she's reading, Dad?" she asked. She moved her horse up beside Brittle and gently shook her daughter's arm. "Abi, Grandad asked you to shut the gate."

Abi blinked her eyes. She hadn't realised she had reached the others.

"Oh," she said. She pushed the e-book back into the saddle bag, then quickly slipped to the ground and shut the gate.

"Which part were you reading, Abi?" Grandad asked as they turned their horses back toward the house. The horses broke into a trot, eager to be home. "The part where Abe Covey decided to stay here. I wonder what it looked like to have sixteen wagons in this meadow?"

"I think it would have looked pretty fine," Grandad said.

"It must have been lonely for him and his wife when the other wagons left,"said Margot. She shivered, not sure if it was the evening air, or the thought of being here alone in the days of wagon trains.

"Here comes that husband of yours," Grandad said.

The sharp, rapid rise of a motor whined through the air like the sound of a giant mosquito. In the distance they could see Dave coming from the house. When he saw them he dropped back a gear and pulled back on the handlebars. The bike's front wheel came up off the ground, and he rode on toward them on the back wheel only.

"Mono!" Abi shouted.

"He'll kill himself that way," Grandad growled. "I've been telling him not to do that since the first time I met him."

Dave circled the horses on his rear wheel, then dropped back onto two and wound the engine down.

"Hurry up!" he called above the sound of the motor. "I've got a meal waiting that's fit for cowboys!" Then he remembered. "I saw Angus, before. The rangers still haven't got that lion. They think it must have gone back into the mountains. They say to keep a watch out in case it comes back." Dave lifted one hand high. "Wagons…ho!" he shouted, and spun the back wheel as he took off.

"You just dug out enough grass to feed a cow for a week!" Grandad roared. "I told you, boy—" Grandad stopped in mid-sentence. Dave would never hear anything above that motor.

"He's as stubborn as—" Grandad began. Then he laughed. He never could stay angry for more than a few moments. "Stubborn as you about your dream, Abi," he finished.

"I only want to do it once," Abi said. "Dad does it every time he gets on his motorbike."

Margot knew what was coming next; but she didn't wait to hear it. She leant

People who won't change their minds are often described as being "as stubborn as a mule." It's well-known that a mule, which is a cross between a donkey and a horse, is hard to move when it wants to stay put.

forward in the saddle, and her long-legged cow pony took the chance to run.

"Hold back, Abi!" Grandad said when she went to follow. "I've got something I want to say while the others aren't here. I've been thinking about your adventure, and I've got an idea."

"What is it?" Abi pleaded. "Quick, Grandad! Tell me!"

"Nope," he said. "That's why I wanted to talk to you alone a moment. I'll bring it up while we're eating tonight, but only if you promise me you'll not say one word, not one word, while your parents and I are talking about it."

"Why?" she demanded. "It's my adventure!"

"And you won't get it for a long time, yet," Grandad snorted. "Not if you talk that way."

Abi shrugged. "I'm sorry," she said. "I won't say anything while you're talking."

"Good," Grandad said smiling to himself. "It's going to be odd having you keep quiet."

Grandad shook Parrish up into a canter, and Abi let Brittle catch up. But her mind was not on the ride. What could Grandad be planning?

chapter 5

Partners in adventure

THAT EVENING they stayed at the farm for dinner. "I've been thinking," Grandad said as they ate. "Thinking about this itch Abe Covey had to see what's on the other side of the mountains."

"What have you been thinking?" Margot said, her voice sharp.

Abi quickly took a mouthful of food so she couldn't speak.

"Well," Grandad said, "except for those five years I was in the army, I've spent my whole life on this place."

"I thought you wanted to," Margot said. "You love the farm."

"Sure I do," Grandad said. "That don't mean I can't have an adventure as well."

"But you've been as far as Abe Covey went several times!" Margot protested.

"You've often said what he tried to do was way too dangerous!"

"Steady, lass," Grandad said gently. "What I've always said was that he was foolish to try that slope. He should have gone back on his tracks and taken another route. He says so himself in the journal. He had a dozen choices. He just happened to be too impatient and he made the wrong one."

Abi felt as though she would burst. It sounded as if Grandad was planning to cross the divide. But surely he wouldn't go without her?

Abi's mouth opened. She just had to speak. Then she saw the look in Grandad's eye, and she snapped her mouth shut again. The look said it would be all over if she broke her promise.

"Well, Abe was younger—you were younger, when you made those trips," Margot said. "You're too old to go up into the mountains again."

"Too old?" Grandad snapped. "Lass, I'm seventy-seven next birthday. Broncho Charlie was eighty-one when he rode from New York to San Francisco. Took him seven months to make that ride. I think I can make a ride of a week or so just outside my own backdoor."

"Who was Broncho Charlie?" Dave asked. "I haven't heard his name before."

"He was the 11-year-old boy who rode for the Pony Express," Grandad said. "Now that was dangerous."

Abi wanted to shout that she was a year older than Broncho Charlie already. But she caught Grandad's eye again, and said nothing.

"I think," said Grandad, "that Abi and myself would make a great pair of adventurers!"

In her mind, Abi shouted "Yey, Grandad!" But she didn't say it out loud.

"She's still too young," Margot said.

"She's too young!" Grandad said. "I'm too old! This is sounding like the story of the three bears. Too hot! Too cold! Well I think the two of us together is just right!"

Margot laughed, suddenly. "You sound like Goldilocks!" she said. "Well...what do you think, Abi?"

Abi looked to Grandad.

"Yup!" he said. "What do you think, Abi?"

Abi leapt to her feet. "Yey, Grandad!" she shouted, and threw her arms around his neck.

In the 1860s, the Pony Express delivered mail, on horseback, between Missouri and California, a distance of 3000 km (1960 miles).

"Well, that sounds kind of positive," said Grandad, grinning broadly.

"Phew," Dave said. "You sure know how to spring a surprise, Grandad. I think Margot and I need to have a good long talk about this."

"While Grandad and I make our plans!" Abi shouted. Suddenly she felt certain they would agree. "Next holidays!" she cried. "In just four weeks!"

"You're certainly not going without a lot of preparation," Margot said. "What if you had an accident? Like Abe Covey."

"He got home!" Abi said.

"He was a very tough man," Margot said. "And even he wouldn't have survived if he'd been much further into his journey."

"You could send a helicopter!" Abi said. "We'll have the CB radio to tell you where we are."

"Do you know how much that would cost?" Margot asked.

"I can take care of the cost of accident insurance," Grandad said.

"You can take my camera," Dave said. "And what about a GPS so you'll be able to tell us exactly where you are? I've been planning to get one for when I'm trail-

The company that started the Pony Express called for "young, skinny, wiry fellows... expert riders, willing to risk their lives for the job. Orphans preferred."

biking. I could get it now and you can take that along, too"

"A what?" Grandad asked.

"A Global Positioning System," Dave explained. "It works from satellites."

"Hey, steady on, boy!" Grandad exclaimed. "We're not taking a wagonload of electronic gear with us. Only what can fit on two packhorses."

"You can hold this in your hand," Dave explained. "It's tiny. It's smaller than a CB radio."

"And it tells you where you are?" Grandad asked.

"Exactly," Dave said. "But, steady on. We haven't said you could go, yet."

"Who, her or me?" Grandad asked.

Dave lifted his hands in surrender. "I give up," he said.

Margot waved a handkerchief.

"We're going, Grandad! We're going!" Abi shouted. She grabbed her e-book. "I'll read you what it says about Abe Covey's start in the journal."

I checked the girth on the packhorse, and then I was ready.

Amelia reminded me of just how long I had waited for that moment. She was

Geo-Positioning Systems (GPS) provide specially coded satellite signals that allow the receiver to pinpoint the exact position of the user.

content for me to go, but she asked me not to be away too long.

Sarah, our new baby, was in her arms, and I kissed them both. Then I squatted down and put my hands on young William's shoulders. I asked him to take care of his mother and sister. He has grown into a fine young boy. He is ten years old, and he thought he should come with me. I would have taken him but I couldn't see Amelia left alone with only the baby. She needs him at home. I told him he could ride with me to the foot of the mountains, and he was back in moments with his pony saddled.

It was hard riding away from my Amelia. We were through the back gate and part-way up the first slope before I stopped the horses and turned to face the distant house. There I leaned over and shook William's hand, and told him again to look after Amelia and the baby.

I watched as he turned his pony and started back for the house. My eyes wandered over the grasslands. They're fenced, now. Cattle graze on them—over a thousand of them, bred from the two hundred we had brought with us. Then I turned the horses. It was time to see the other side of the mountains.

Periodically, cattle are rounded up and brought back to the homestead so they can be tagged or branded or prepared for sale.

39

Two days into my journey, now. I've brought some sheets so I can keep my journal up to date. It's peaceful, up here. I can hear the sound of the two horses grazing on the mountain grass. They're outside the circle of light cast by the fire, so I need to listen now and then to be sure they've not strayed.

The hobbles will keep the packhorse from going too far, and the Arab won't wander away from me. I'll bring them in and tether them before I bed down, just in case of lions.

Arabian horses are well-known for their stamina. During the Crimean War, an Arabian horse galloped 155 km (93 miles) without injury. Its rider, however, died from exhaustion!

I'm beginning to see that Joe Feather was right not to try and find a way over the mountains for the wagons. They're much steeper than they look from the plains. Right now I'm on a patch of grass, but I can't be sure how the feed will be beyond. Before the sun went down I checked the way ahead. The mountains rise quite suddenly again on all sides, except the one I came in by. I have a feeling I should go back down my own trail for a day or two, and try another way, but I'm impatient and that would add quite some time to my journey.

In the morning I'll try the horses on one of the slopes and see if they can manage the climb.

chapter 6
Wagons...ho!

"I'M EXHAUSTED!" Dave said as he made breakfast on the morning the adventure was to begin.

The past four weeks had seen each one of them spending their spare time planning and putting together all that was to be taken on the trek to the top of the mountains.

Now they were ready, and as Abi finished each mouthful of breakfast she would suddenly lift a fist into the air and cry: "Wagons...ho!"

"You should've been born a hundred years ago," Margot said. "You're wasted in the twenty-first century."

"Oh, I don't know," Grandad said. "Give her a few more years and she might be leading some mission to the stars. Adventurers fit themselves to their times and places. If Abe Covey were alive today, he'd be looking to the stars."

"I just want to look over the top of the mountains!" Abi said. "Are we ready?"

"I guess so," Grandad said.

"Wagons...ho!" Abi shouted again, and ran for the door.

They put the pack-saddles on Wagon Boss and Rebel, first. And even though they had checked the gear the night before, Margot insisted on an extra check.

"You're more fortunate than Abe Covey," Margot said as checked the list. "You have the GPS. He only had the sun and the stars to tell him where he was. You've got the CB to keep in touch and call for help if you need it. He had no way of calling for help except a gunshot; and that can only be heard for a short distance. He couldn't get medical help when he needed it, but you could even get a helicopter with a doctor if you needed to." Margot checked through the first-aid kit. "I wonder what Abe would have used for pain," she said as she checked the tablets. "Or antiseptic."

"You make it sound as if we're just going on a picnic," Grandad said. "An adventure should have some risk."

Morphine, which was the most common painkiller used by doctors in the 1800s, comes from the dried resin of the opium poppy.

"But only acceptable risk!" Margot snapped. "Even Abe Covey would have taken every precaution he could to make it a safe trip."

"Well, we have too!" Abi said quickly. She felt a sudden panic that Margot would suddenly change her mind and stop the expedition right now.

"Yes, you have," Margot agreed, and Abi gave a little sigh of relief. But it still seemed an age before the last bag was strapped shut, and they were ready to put the saddles onto the riding horses.

Margot and Dave were going with them for part of the first day, although Dave said he would give them a head start. He stayed back to clear up, while the others rode out at sunrise.

Margot's horse, Logie Girl, was being skittish. The wounds were well healed, but maybe the saddle reminded her of the lion clutched to her back. Margot eased her along, talking quietly to calm her.

A commonly used riding saddle.

Five horses, three riders, moving at a steady jog across the meadows, the tops of the mountains already in full sunlight.

"Westward," Grandad said as they rode. "It's like following the sun."

From where they rode across the

meadow they could see the highest parts of the mountains. But they knew that when they were in the mountains they would not be able to see the high points until they had almost reached them.

The mountain range was not a single slope leading from the bottom to the top. It was a series of rising hills with steep valleys in between. The valleys mostly ran north and south, so they could not follow them, but would have to cut across them. Perhaps from the crests of some of the hills they would be able to see the high points of the mountains, but in the valleys they would see nothing but the hillside ahead

Margot brought Logie Girl closer. "Test your CB, Abi," she said.

Abi slipped the CB from the saddlebag, and switched it on.

"Westward Ho to base," she said into the microphone. "Westward Ho to base."

The sound of something breaking came from the speaker. "Damn!" Dave's voice said. "Yeah, Abi?"

"What was that?" Abi asked.

"I got a fright and dropped a glass."

"I just thought I should check and see if it was working," Abi said.

"It's working fine," Dave answered. "Except I had the volume up too loud. Now let me get on with my housework so I can follow you."

Margot laughed and Logie Girl shied. "Steady! Steady!" Margot soothed. "It's going to be a long time before she forgets that lion."

"They never spend the night down here anymore," Grandad said.

Abi slipped the CB back into the saddle bag as she crossed the cottonwood stream. She was leading the packhorse, Wagon Boss. He tugged at the lead, and threw his head up. Abi halted Brittle on the far bank while the packhorse drank.

When Wagon Boss finished, Abi tugged his lead. He waded across the creek after them, and Abi hurried Brittle to catch up with the others.

At the far back of the farm there was a wooden gate. Abi pulled her e-book from the saddle bag. "Wooden gate..." she murmured, as she searched for one of the earliest entries in the journal.

This saddle is used for cattle work. The end of a lasso can be tied to the horn at the front so the horse as well as the rider can take the strain of holding the lassoed beast.

Today I strung the last of the wire fence across the western boundary of our land. Right in the centre I have set two large posts. Each night in the barn, for the past few weeks, I've been working on building a wooden gate. I've taken special care with it. This is the gateway to our journey to the other side of the mountains.

Wagons were covered with canvas stretched across iron rods that were arched over the timber frame. Whole families travelled and slept in a wagon together.

I've long since taken the cover off our wagon so it can be used to haul lumber and other goods. The four oxen who hauled us here are of little use now. We have four fine heavy-horses to haul it. The oxen should rightly be used for meat and hide, but we have a strong affection for them in bringing us here safely, so we leave them to a peaceful old age on our meadows. The four horses make a journey to town quite rapid. We can reach it in a week, now.

Last night I got the finished gate up onto the wagon. Come midday, Amelia harnessed two of the horses, and with baby William in his box behind the seat, came out to have lunch with me. Then she stayed to watch while I swung the gate for the first time. It was cause for celebration.

None of them ever opened the wooden gate in the back fence without thinking of that entry in Abe Covey's journal. They often came here to let the cattle out to graze in the foothills of the mountains. The grass was good, and it kept the foothills safer from wildfire. But no matter how often they used it, the gate was still special.

"I'm never going to let you take that e-book with you after you learn to drive," Margot said. "No vehicle is going to steer itself while you dream."

"Brittle knows where to go," Abi said. She put the e-book back into the saddle bag and swung down and lifted the wooden tongue that kept the gate closed.

"Leave it open for your father, Abi," Grandad said. "There're no cattle in this pasture today."

The land began to rise quite steeply at this point. The fir trees that were dense higher in the mountains, were spread out here. It left plenty of open land for grass. The cattle liked it in summer when they had the shade of the fir trees to rest in.

Grandad led the way, leaning forward in his saddle as the horse climbed.

They reached the top of the first rise around lunchtime. Grandad brought his horses to a halt. "Lunch here?" he asked.

The others agreed, and dismounted, tethering the horses as the sound of a motorbike came from below.

Margot collected twigs and fir cones and made a fire. Abi got the iron triangle and pot from one of the pack-saddles, and filled the pot with water. Then Grandad set the triangle above the new flames and he was just hanging the pot to boil as the motorbike arrived.

Dave had made lunch for this first stop. They set it out in the shade of a big fir tree. While they ate, Dave wandered around with the camera to make a record of the start of the journey.

They came up here occasionally to picnic. Below them the farm spread out like a picture in a book. It seemed to Abi that if she leaned forward far enough she would be able to pick the cattle up and move them around.

Only Margot was not relaxed. She didn't say anything, but Abi knew she was still worried about the days ahead.

"I've got something else for you," Dave said when they had finished the meal. He went to his motorbike and took a roll of paper from one of the saddle bags. "I enlarged a copy of Abe Covey's map. It only shows the way as far as his accident, but it might be useful."

He unrolled it for them to study.

"Gives us a good start," Grandad said. "Also tells us where not to go." He tipped the coffee grounds from his mug and stood up. "Let's move this adventure on!"

"Hooray!" Abi cried. She re-rolled the map and ran for the horses.

"Be careful!" Margot called.

"Good luck!" Dave shouted as Abi and Grandad disappeared into the firs.

The warm scent of the horses mixed with the smell of leather and fir trees. The horses tossed their heads as they went, as if they knew this was a different venture to their usual cattle work.

That evening, Abi took out a school exercise book to make the first entry in her own journal:

First Camp of the Famous Grandad and Abi Expedition into the Mountains!

We are right where Abe Covey made his first stop. Grandad has been here before. He worked out the way from Abe Covey's map.

After we left Mum and Dad at the picnic spot, we climbed over the first ridge, then made our way up a long valley. Then we climbed another ridge, and stopped there to rest the horses and call back to base camp. Dad had told me the radio waves might not get out of the deep valleys, so it would be best to call from the ridges.

While Grandad got the fire going, I took the horses along the valley and found a pool for them to drink from. There was no stream there, so I think the pool must fill up from a spring, or maybe rain. After they finished drinking, I tied them to different trees so they could each have plenty of grass. Then I came back and heaped up fir needles for Grandad and me to sleep on.

Now we're going to eat! You get very hungry when you're on an expedition!

The jingle and crunch of horses hooves and gear came to a stop. It was the evening of the second day. They had reached the point where Abe Covey had marked the X on his map. It was the place where his leg had been smashed in the accident and he'd had to turn back. From this point on they would have to find their own way.

A currycomb is used to clean a horse's coat.

Abi swung down from the saddle, but Grandad took longer.

"Getting stiff in my old age," he said.

They pulled the saddles off, and swapped the bridles for halters with tether ropes on them. Already they had worked out the best way to make camp.

A bodybrush helps to make a horse's coat shine.

Abi gave each horse a quick rub down. The sweat from under the saddles could chill the horses, or start sore patches if it was not dried off. Then she put an X into the search box of the e-book, and read the entry she needed:

I will bring my map up to date, before bedding down. You will note an X on the path I used. I suggest anyone following this map should try another way. While the path leads to a grassy patch, there is no easy way beyond it.

Abi unrolled the map and checked it. "I'll go and find that grassy patch Abe Covey said is here," Abi said. She climbed onto Brittle's bare back, and held the ropes of all four horses bunched in one hand. Grandad already had a camp fire started. He handed the water pot up to Abi.

"Don't be too long," he said. "A man is perishing for a drink."

Abi guided Brittle up into the valley Abe Covey had marked on his map all those years ago. Not far along, just as Abe had marked it, there was good grass and a small stream.

Abi let the horses drink, then slipped off Brittle's back and tethered them all where they could feed. Then she dipped the pot into the stream above, and ran back down the valley to Grandad.

"Show you how to make a simple bread," Grandad said. He tipped some flour into the bottom of a small pot, then added salt. "You can put in fancy stuff like dried fruit, it you want," he said. "But just flour and salt is good enough."He tipped some water from the pot onto the flour, and mixed it up into a stiff dough. Then he clamped on the lid and pushed it in among the coals.

While dinner was cooking, Abi got out her sleeping bag and Grandad's blankets, her mind drifting into the past. She didn't need her e-book to remember this part...

It was very early in the morning when I set out to climb to the next ridge. I know now I should have turned back and tried another way. The two horses climbed well until near the top. Then the packhorse stumbled in a hole. It drove my mount into a tree. Neither animal was hurt, but my left leg was crushed and torn open.

It's a year since this took place. I did not wish to write about it until now.

When it happened I had no choice but to turn my mount around. We reached the bottom of the slope somehow, but I was faint, by then. I pulled the packhorse to me and, leaning across, took the straps and ropes from it and used them to bind myself to the saddle as best I could. There was no chance for me if I ended up on the ground.

I managed to lean forward far enough to get the bridle off; and from then on it was up to my horse. The crushing of my leg and the loss of blood had taken all my strength. I must have passed out of consciousness many times. I remember urging my horse on, whenever I could. The rest I cannot recall.

How long the journey home took, I do not know. My horse kept moving, even through the night.

One morning I woke and found he was standing at my wooden gate. There was no chance that I could open it. No chance that my wife or son would come this way and find me.

With the last of my strength I pulled the gun from the saddle, and shot it into the air.

My next memory is of looking up into the eyes of my Amelia.

Now, one year on, I can hobble about well enough. But I will never see beyond the mountains now.

"Why those tears, Abi?" Grandad asked gently.

Abi looked across at him through the firelight. The tears seemed to splinter the flames.

"I was…"

"No," he said. "No need to say. I was thinking of him, too."

They were both quiet for several moments. Then Grandad hooked the pot out of the coals and flicked off the lid.

"It smells good, Grandad," Abi said. She wiped away the tears.

"Then let's eat," Grandad said. "Soon as that's done we can call in our position, and get to bed. We have some mountains to climb!"

They were hardly in bed when one of the horses whinnied in fright.

"Not that lion again!" Grandad snapped, throwing his blankets off and snatching up the carbine.

Abi was tangled in her sleeping bag, and by the time she got her boots on Grandad had already gone. She ran after him through the dark, stumbling on the unfamiliar ground. She almost fell when the sound of the crashing gunshot caught her by surprise, so much louder here in the mountains than it would have been on the plain.

Carbines are particularly useful in difficult terrain or when movement is restricted because they are automatic and lightweight, making them easy to handle.

"Grandad?" she called.

"Just a frightening shot!" he called back. "Come and help me get the horses! If it is that critter, it will have spooked them bad. They'll be remembering that night on the cottonwood stream!"

"Could it really be the same lion?" she asked as she ran up to him.

"Yup!" Grandad answered. "Ah, devil it!" he continued as the sudden sound of breaking branches and crashing brush came from ahead. "One's away. Never catch him in the night."

Abi had a sudden terrible vision of the adventure ending right there. If any one of the horses got away, they would have to go back. They could not leave a pack-saddle behind and go on. They needed everything they had brought. And once Mum knew even one thing had gone awry, she would never let them start out again.

She burst away into the night in the direction of the sound.

"Abi!" Grandad roared. "Come back here!"

She pretended not to hear, and dodged on among the dark firs. Her eyes were young, and she could see more than her grandfather could. She could hear from ahead the sound of something being dragged, and guessed it was the branch of the fir she had tied the bolted horse to.

Grandad was still calling to her from behind, but she continued to ignore

him and follow the sound of the horse
and the dragged branch.

The further she ran, the easier she
found it to see. After a few minutes the
horse seemed to slow. The branch would
be catching against trees as it went; and
the panic would be easing. Maybe it was
Brittle, she thought suddenly.

Abi stopped and called. The noises
came to a sudden halt, and she called
again. She was answered by a frightened
whinny.

It was Brittle! She was sure.

Abi continued on in the same direction,
and suddenly she could see the dark
shape of a horse ahead.

It was only then that she remembered
the lion. Perhaps it had dropped onto
Brittle's back. Perhaps it was still stalking
the horse...

Goose bumps sprang up on Abi's skin.
She spun around to go back. But if the
lion was there...and the trailing tether and
branch trapped Brittle, her horse would
have no chance of avoiding an attack.

As quickly as she had turned away, she
turned back and ran, screaming the
horse's name as she went; hoping the
sound of a human voice would frighten

the lion if it was still about.

"Brittle!" She didn't wait to free the tether from the branch, but snapped the catch off his halter and clawed her way up onto his back. "Go!"

The horse took no urging, but burst away in a panic between the trees. Abi lay out along his back, trying to guide him as the low branches of the firs whipped against her.

"Grandad!" she screamed to find a direction.

His voice came from somewhere to the left. She turned Brittle toward it, and slowed him. "Steady, steady, steady..."

As the panic left Abi, the horse felt the change and slowed until it was moving at a trot.

"I've got him, Grandad!" she shouted. "I've got Brittle!"

By the time Abi reached Grandad he had the ropes of the other three horses in his hands. He didn't speak to her as she slipped to the ground, and she knew he was angry.

Grandad led the horses back to the camp, and began to tie them. Finally he spoke to her.

"Are you ever going to disobey me

again when I give you an order?"

"No," Abi whispered.

"Because if you think you might, then we're turning round first thing tomorrow morning and going home."

"I won't, Grandad," she whispered. "Never, ever, again. I know it was stupid to do what I just did."

"Tether your horse," Grandad said. He built up the fire, but he didn't speak, and his silent anger was far worse than if he had been shouting.

Abi tethered Brittle on another rope, and crept back to the fire. Grandad handed her a cup of hot chocolate, and sat back on his heels, still silent. Slowly, Abi edged across until she was right beside him. Then she put out her hand, and held his.

"I'm sorry," she whispered. There were tears in her eyes.

Grandad gave a deep sigh, then he took her hand in his. "It sure was stupid, what you did," he said. "But it showed courage, too. Just learn to know the difference, and you'll venture to the stars yet, my girl."

They sat there, side by side, just listening to the night.

The horses were still snorting from time to time, but settling slowly. An owl hooted from somewhere, and they could hear crickets all around.

"Must have been that old lame lion," Grandad said. "Can't think of anything else that would spook them." He was quiet a moment, then went on: "Don't think we need tell the others, though. No sense worrying them."

The next morning they took a different path to the one Abe Covey had taken. They could see why he had tried the way he had. It was obviously shorter.

Owls have to turn their whole head to look sideways. This is because their eyes are surrounded by a capsule made of bone.

The way they chose was on an angle to the north. It led them to an easier climb to the next ridge.

The mountains rose in a series of steps. Each ridge was higher than the next, but there was always a valley beyond which took them down before the next climb.

Each night they kept the horses in close to where they camped, and each night they called in on the CB and gave their new position.

"We're plotting your journey on a

map," Dave said over the radio.

"You're only getting the end-of-the-day points," Grandad said. "Truth is, we're zigzagging all over the place to find the best way."

"Just keep being careful," Margot always ended.

It seemed strange to Abi to be chatting to them in the kitchen of the farmhouse, while she and Grandad were camped in a different place each night. She was glad Mum and Dad didn't know that sometime during each night the horses would begin to whinny and snort, and that it wasn't until Grandad fired a shot into the air, that they calmed.

The lion was following them. They were sure.

chapter 7

Disaster and disappointment

"You know," Grandad said, as they camped for the sixth night. "Looks to me as if we've only got one more climb."

Abi looked upwards to the top of the next ridge. Or was it the top of the mountains? She certainly couldn't see anything beyond but that was usual in the valleys.

"Dad! Mum!" she said into the CB when she called to report. "We think we might be there by tomorrow!"

"Sure looks like it from here," Grandad chipped in.

"And you will have reached your dream!" Dave said.

"And we might get some peace at last!" Margot added.

"We're going to start even earlier tomorrow!" Abi said. "Good night!"

"Good night," said Margot and Dave together.

In the morning, Abi had the fire lit before Grandad was even awake.

"In a hurry, Abi?" Grandad asked.

"I've been waiting for this all my life!" Abi cried.

They moved out as soon as it was light enough to see the way clearly.

Abi hurried Brittle forward; but Grandad made her slow down.

"Just take it nice and easy," he said. "Rushing just brings risk. We don't want to risk anything now we're right on the edge of reaching our goal."

It was a steady climb, but a long one. Wagon Boss kept wanting to stop and feed, and Abi had trouble moving him along. She wanted to reach the top at the same time as Grandad; but the packhorse kept on being difficult, and Grandad crested the ridge first.

"Ah, shame it!" Grandad said as Parrish reached the ridge.

"What?" Abi called, dropping the line to Wagon Boss, and urging Brittle forward.

With a last heave, Brittle came up beside Parrish and stopped. Abi leaned forward to look.

"Oh, Grandad," she said in disappointment.

It wasn't the last climb after all. Between them and that last, easy slope, was a deep valley. And to get through the valley, they must go down a barren slope of slippery shale.

"Doesn't look good," said Grandad.

"It won't stop us, will it?" Abi asked urgently.

Grandad ran his eyes along the slope. "Doesn't seem to be any better along either way," he said.

They looked across the valley. The top of the other side was the top of the mountains, they were sure. It was their goal, and from it they would be able to see what Abe Covey had wanted to see all those years ago.

But the steep slope ahead of them was a barrier. A real barrier.

"Well, Abi. What do you think?" Grandad asked.

"We can't stop now," Abi said. "We have to reach the top. We have to!"

Grandad looked each way again, and

shook his head. "It's not going to
be easy."

"But we can do it" Abi said. "Look at
what we've done already."

Grandad nodded. "Let's turn along the
ridge and see if the slope gets easier
somewhere along the way."

"Which direction?" Abi asked,
tightening the reins.

"North," Grandad said.

The top of the ridge was nearly flat,
and well wide enough for the horses. But
the loose shale made it dangerous to go
faster than a walk. The horses snorted
and threw their heads about as they
went. They didn't like moving over such
a risky surface.

As they rode, Grandad and Abi
watched the slope to their left. But it got
no easier. After a couple of hours
Grandad called a halt.

"We need to decide right now to go
down, or go home," he said.

"Down!" Abi said. "We can't get this
close and give up!"

"Okay then, Abi. Best make a radio
report from here. The valley floor looks a
good place to camp on the way back. But
they won't receive us from there."

A scraper is
used to
remove
sweat from
a horse so it
doesn't get
cold.

"Okay," Abi said.

She took the CB from its pocket, and then the GPS.

"I'll check the saddles while you do that," Grandad said, dismounting. "Can't afford to have anything slip, going down a slope like this."

Abi switched on the CB. "Westward Ho to base," she called.

The answer was almost immediate. Mum must have been in the kitchen.

"Abi! Have you reached the top? What can you see?"

"We were wrong," Abi said. "There was another ridge and a valley. We're going down in a few minutes."

"Oh, Abi!" Margot said. "What a disappointment."

"It's all right," Abi said. "The floor of the valley looks like a good place to camp on our way back. We'll probably leave the packhorses and gear there while we go on to the top. It's a very deep valley. The CB might not work from the bottom, so we thought we should report from here." She checked the position on the GPS, and read it out.

Mum repeated it to check.

"Tell us when you get there," Margot

The fleshy underside of a horse's hoof is called the frog.

said. "And Abi, be very careful!"

"We will," Abi said.

She moved her left leg so Grandad could get at the girth strap to check it.

"All shipshape and fair to go!" Grandad said. He remounted Parrish.

Abi raised her arm and punched the air. "Let's ride!" she cried.

They turned their horses, and leaned back in the saddles. All four of the horses were sure-footed, and the two riders let them pick their own way down.

"Be easier coming back up," Grandad said as they rode. "Climbing gives them a better balance. Be real careful, Abi."

Abi nodded but didn't speak. The way Brittle's hooves kept slipping on the shale frightened her. She didn't want to end the adventure by falling. Not when they were so close to their goal.

But, what did happen, shocked her. Somehow she had never thought of anything happening to Grandad.

They were right near the flat land at the bottom of the valley. Abi was already looking about for the best place to camp; although perhaps it didn't really matter. The grass was green everywhere, and

Horse shoes protect the horse's hooves from becoming soft and chipping away. They also give the horse better grip on unstable surfaces.

would give the horses the best grazing since they had left the farm. Even from a distance she could see there were waterholes along the bed of the stream, they would be able to drink until they were full. The firs would make a cosy place to camp, and there would be an abundance of fir cones for a hot, bright fire.

She let her mind wander ahead, and chose a place for her sleeping bag under a small, dense fir. They always chose small firs, now they knew the lion was following. Trees that were too small for it to climb into.

"Whoa-up!" Grandad shouted.

Abi swung round just in time to see Rebel slip. The horse lurched to one side and his heavy pack-saddle slammed into Grandad. There was a dull, snapping sound. Then Rebel regained his balance and dropped his head to feed.

"I thought he was going to knock you down!" Abi called as she reached the flat ground.

She slipped from the saddle. Then she tethered the packhorse to a fir.

"Come on, Grandad!" Abi called.

Often, horses are set loose wearing a headstall so that they can be caught easily when needed.

It was only then she realised something was wrong. Grandad sat with his hands gripping the saddle. He was staring straight ahead, his jaw clamped shut.

"Grandad?" Abi asked without moving. "Grandad? What's wrong?"

He neither spoke nor moved.

"Grandad!" Abi screamed. She ran to him and snatched Parrish's bridle. She looked up into her grandfather's face. His eyes moved down to her. But it seemed to take him an age before he could unclamp his teeth.

Grandad took a deep breath, then shook his head to clear it. "Rebel broke my leg, Abi," he whispered at last.

chapter 8
Abi takes control

THE WHOLE VALLEY seemed to sway in front of Abi's eyes. She reached for the saddle to stop herself falling. Then her eyes cleared and the strange feeling went away.

"I'll get help," she managed. She jerked Grandad's CB from his saddle. "I'll go back to the ridge!"

"No!" he said through gritted teeth.

"We can't ride back," Abi cried.

"No," he agreed. "Abe had to do that, or die. We don't. But they won't bring a helicopter in this late at night."

"We have to do something!" Abi cried.

"Yup," he said. "You have to get a splint on this leg of mine. Then you're going on up to look over the top. I'm not going anywhere till you get to see what Abe Covey wanted to see."

"That doesn't matter anymore!" she cried. "We just have to get a doctor!" Abi's eyes filled with tears

"No time for crying, Abi," Grandad said. "Just tie my horse while you make me up a good, soft bed. Then we'll get this leg splinted up, and I'll get onto the bed. I'll lay easy with a good heap of needles under the blankets, and a dose of them pain-killers."

"Let me call the doctor first?" Abi begged.

"I said no, Abi!" Grandad snapped. He gritted his teeth as the pain gripped him. "You do what I tell you. I'm not sitting in this saddle for hours, and we're not leaving this valley till you've climbed this mountain!"

"I don't care about the mountain!" Abi sobbed.

"Move!" he roared. "I'm in high pain!"

Abi's whole body was shaking with sobs, but she led Parrish and Rebel to a fir and tethered them.

"Heap up some needles and get my blankets laid out," Grandad said softly.

Abi dropped to her knees and scooped up armfuls of fir needles The sobbing left her body as she worked, and when the tears stopped she wiped her eyes dry on her sleeves.

"Not such a disaster," Grandad said softly from the saddle. "You won't even need a horse to go the last way. If something like this had happened further down, you would never have seen over.

"I want you up there on the ridge as the sun sets. You can call them on the CB from there. Then I want you to see what Abe Covey wished all his life he could see. Then I want you to come back down here and tell me everything you saw."

"I will, Grandad! I will!" Abi promised.

She unbuckled the saddle from Rebel, and pulled it onto the ground. Then she took the straps from around the blankets, and lay two on top of the bed of needles.

"We don't have any splints!" she said.

"Sure we do," Grandad said. "You just think that's a pot hanger. Unclip its legs—with some padding, and a lot of bandaging, it'll make up a fine splint.

"War wasn't just shooting at people, Abi. It was looking after people, too. We taught ourselves a lot of first aid in the army. Taught ourselves to make do with what we had right there until the medics came. I've helped fix up a lot worse than

a broken leg with much less than we have
here."

"You...you're wonderful, Grandad,"
Abi whispered. "And you're brave!"

She got the blackened pot hanger they
used to put over the fire, and
unclipped the three legs.

"Now wrap some clothing around
my leg to pad it," Grandad said.

"Your leg's bleeding!" Abi cried.

"It's not bad," Grandad said. "Come
on now!"

Grandad leaned down, and working
together they bound the three metal
legs from the pot hanger into a firm
splint about his leg.

"Now turn Parrish about, and bring
him right alongside that bed," Grandad
said. "Then you're going to help me
fall right down onto it."

Abi turned the horse and stood him
beside the bed.

"Now get my foot out of the stirrup,"
Grandad told her.

A choked snarl came from Grandad
as Abi eased his boot from the stirrup.

"I hurt you!" she cried.

"Everything hurts right now!" he
roared. "I'm going to make some terrible

noises when I hit that bed. But you just go about getting me some hot coffee and pain-killers while I settle."

Grandad leaned far forward in the saddle, and got a good grip of the leather on each side.

"Now! I'm going to swing my good leg over, and cling here to the saddle while you get my bad leg out of the way. Then I'm going to let go and fall."

Grandad swung his good leg over. Abi could not remember very much of the next few moments. She knew she must have moved his leg. And she could remember putting it gently beside the other leg when he was down. But that was all.

Parrish pulled back and away as Grandad fell, and Abi had to go and catch the horse and calm him. She couldn't look at Grandad yet, and she knew he wouldn't want her to until he had himself under control.

Abi took off the other horses' saddles and put hobbles on all four horses. Next, a fire for Grandad's coffee. There was a chill in the valley air, so she made the fire close to Grandad's bed. He was making some terrible sounds. But Abi knew he

Hobbles are a rope or strap placed around a horse's front legs so it can move enough to graze, but can't run away.

didn't want her to say anything.

She built the fire of twigs and needles, and when it was crackling, fed dried fir cones into it. While they were catching she dug a trench through the needles to the earth. It went right to the damp earth, so there was no chance of the fire burning through to Grandad's bedding.

Then she ran down to the creek. The waterholes were dark and gloomy in the valley's shadows. The water spooked her, and she dipped the pot and ran.

"Coffee in a minute," she called to Grandad, speaking to him for the first time since he had left the saddle.

"Need it, too," Grandad managed.

With the pot hanger being used as a splint, Abi had to set the pot on the ground against the fire—but it wouldn't take long to boil as many of the fir cones were already glowing.

She got the painkillers from the first-aid kit, read the directions, and broke two from their foil wrapping.

"Can I put some blankets over you now, Grandad?" she whispered.

"Thank you, Abi," he answered gently.

"I'll get you some water, so you can take the tablets with it."

Abi gently covered Grandad with two blankets. Then she worked a saddle under his shoulders and helped him take the tablets.

"That's better," he whispered. "I'm settling now, so you can get on up the mountain and give them a call. Just get me that hot coffee to have while you're away."

Abi picked up the CB radio and GPS.

"Load the carbine and put it beside me," he said. "You better lay it right here beside me so I can fire it if I need you in a hurry. I'm not moving so well."

She loaded the carbine and set it where he could easily reach it.

"Now you remember, Abi. I want to know everything you see when you reach our goal. Everything."

Abi ran down to the stream, and crossed on a rock ledge between the waterholes. Then she ran as far as the stream flats went. After that the slope was too steep for running.

She made her way up through the firs. It took about an hour before the trees thinned, and felt she was high enough for a radio signal to get out from the CB.

"Westward Ho to base," she called.

The answer was almost immediate: "Made it?" Dave's voice came. "Are you on the ridge?"

Abi wiped the sudden rush of tears from her eyes, and tried to make her voice normal.

"Dad...Grandad had an accident. One of his legs is broken. Oh, Dad, quick! You've got to get a helicopter here!"

Dave's voice stayed cool, but it had a shake in it. "Tell us exactly what has happened, Abi."

"It was because of the slope," she said. "Rebel stumbled and his pack hit Grandad. He can't stand up or anything. And he's in terrible pain. He's lying on a bed of needles at the bottom of the valley. There's room for a helicopter to land."

"Okay," Dave said. "Give us your exact position."

Abi read the position from the GPS. "Grandad is almost exactly halfway between this position and the last one I gave you. Please hurry!"

It was Margot who answered Abi.

"As quickly as we can," she said. "Just keep your CB switched on."

"I don't think it will get a signal in the valley," Abi answered.

A broken bone will not mend properly unless the bone is set straight and the limb is immobilised with a plaster cast.

"Keep it switched on anyway," Margot answered. "And keep Grandad warm."

Abi just nodded at the CB. Then she looked at the ridge above, and back to the valley below. She wanted to go straight back to Grandad, but he had said...

She turned and scrambled up the last of the slope, and stood at last on the highest point of the mountains.

Her eyes misted. She could almost feel the spirit of Abe Covey take control. Her eyes didn't see what was there now; they saw what Abe would have seen in 1867 if he'd succeeded.

Down below, and for as far beyond as the eye could see, stretched an endless plain of grasslands. A mighty river ran through the plains, with streams leading into it. Cattle country. Farming country. Riverboat country. Enough good land to feed the people of several cities. Enough country on which to build a million dreams. The kind of land Abe had always hoped would lie beyond the mountains.

Then the misting left Abi's eyes, and she saw that the dreams she knew Abe Covey would have had for those plains 133 years ago had come true.

Now they were criss-crossed with

roads and railways. A city and towns had been built. There was an airport and a river port. Great open parks were dotted around the city, and surrounding it all were endless stretches of farmland.

Abi smiled to herself. This is what the pioneers had gone to find. New places for the people of the world's overcrowded cities, where space and food and shelter were not a luxury for the lucky few, but shared by everyone.

She turned, suddenly happy and eager to tell Grandad, and started back down the valley.

The old lion was desperately hungry. It edged toward the horses as silently as its lame leg would allow. But it could not hide its own scent, which drifted ahead of it. The horses could smell it. They whinnied in fear and moved away as best they could with their hobbled forelegs.

The lion stopped, its tail lashing in frustrated anger. Then it caught the scent of the wounded man and turned its head. For several moments it sniffed the air, then it turned in the direction of the smell of new blood.

chapter 9
The final climb

ABI HURRIED. But even though she was going downhill it seemed an age before she was at the stream again, and within sight of the camp.

The lion had reached it before her. It had stopped for several minutes within a single bound of Grandad—watching, testing the air—the scent of blood driving out the fear of man as hunger bit into its belly.

Abi reached the stream. From here she would be able to see...

"Grandad!" she screamed. "Grandad!"

The lion's head jerked up.

Abi skidded on the stones as she hurried to cross the stream.

"Grandad!"

She could see the lion hunched, ready to spring.

"Grandad!" Abi's screeching voice echoed around her.

The lion sniffed the air, then focused on its prey again. As Abi called out one more time, Grandad dragged himself back to consciousness, his hand automatically lifting the carbine.

The lion sprang.

Abi slipped and crashed to her face.

The gunshot woke angry echoes in the valley.

The lion thudded down on top of the man.

"Grandad!" Abi sobbed as she regained her feet and ran on. "Oh, Grandad!"

She felt no fear at all as she caught the lion about its neck and jerked to haul it away. It came, limp; and only then did she realise it was dead.

"Never did like to kill," Grandad whispered. "But it was him or me. Now make a man another hot coffee."

She nodded, her mouth trembling too much for speech. She built up the fire, and got fresh water, then tried to drag the lion away. But it was too heavy for her, and she wondered how she had found the strength to move it when she had thought it was trying to kill her grandfather.

"Leave it be," Grandad said. "Two old-timers with their legs bust in. Take a photograph of us for me to hang in the kitchen to remind me. Then tell me what's over the mountains."

Abi took the photograph, then sat close beside him. "It's wonderful on the other side," she said. "Abe Covey would have seen an endless plain of grassland. He would have loved it, Grandad. He could have had the biggest cattle range there ever was. There are streams, everywhere, all leading to a huge river."

"Riverboats!" Grandad said softly. "If I know our Abe, he would have built a home somewhere on that river. Then he would have built a paddle-steamer, and gone trading."

"He would have gone trading right down to the sea!" Abi said.

Suddenly they were able to laugh.

"It's in the blood," Grandad said.

The CB crackled, but they couldn't make out what the voice was saying.

"I'll take it up the ridge," Abi said.

A short way up the slope she stopped and called home.

"Abi!" Margot's voice came back. "We've been trying to get you."

"Is the doctor coming?" Abi asked.

"No," Margot said, her voice worried. "They won't fly in there at night unless you think Grandad is…is going to die."

"He's not!" Abi cried.

"They say they'll come in at sunrise. You're going to have to look after him for the whole night."

"But he's in pain!" Abi cried. "They have to come now!"

"It's too dangerous," Margot said. "It's not like a pick-up on the plains."

"But it's not night yet!" Abi shouted.

"It would be by the time they got there," Dave said. "Abi, you have to be brave."

"I can handle it!" Abi cried. "I'm not worried for me! I'm worried for Grandad!"

"Then do your best to make it easy for him tonight," Margot said softly. "You'll get help first thing in the morning."

"All right," Abi whispered.

"And leave your CB on," Dave said.

Back at the camp Abi cooked an evening meal. Grandad seemed to rest more easily after they had eaten.

"Just because we've got troubles doesn't mean we change our habits, Abi," he said after the meal. "Time to set down the day's happenings."

Abi got the journal from the saddle bag, and sat up close to Grandad. She had to work by firelight, but she had done that often enough on the trip. The journal had grown over the time they had been on their adventure.

She pulled the top off the pen and began to write:

An unattended campfire can become a devastating forestfire, burning a whole forest bare within hours.

I feel like Abe Covey must have felt after his accident. I just don't want to write about what happened to Grandad. The difference is that his accident stopped Abe Covey ever seeing his dream; but Grandad's didn't stop me.

It was a beautiful sight. It was odd, too, because at first I saw it the way Abe Covey would have seen it all those years ago. I suppose my mind made it up from old photographs I've seen in

Grandad's albums. But it looked real.

I wonder what it will look like in another 133 years?

I've got to find something else I really want to do now I've seen over the top of the mountains. For years I've wanted to do that. But now that I've seen it, I want something new to plan. I want to see over the horizon. I want to see everything there is to see.

Grandad said one day I might go to the stars. I think I might, too. I want to do heaps of things!

It's getting dark, now. The horses are all hobbled. I will bring them in and tether them in a minute. It's going to be scary going back down the mountain by myself. I don't think Grandad's thought of that, but I know I can do it. I have plenty of food for the trip home. It will be just as slow as coming up because of the valleys. Next time I go on an adventure I want to be able to go back by a different route, but there's no choice here. I'd have to go down the other side of the mountains, and then around. But that would take a year.

Abi stopped writing and gazed into the fire for several moments. Then she put the journal back into the saddle bag.

"I think I'll go and get the horses, now," she said.

"Leave them," Grandad told her. He touched the soft pelt of the lion beside him. "With this poor critter out of the way, they'll be safe, tonight. If you'll just pull this saddle out from under my shoulders, I might try for some sleep."

First light touched the peaks of the mountains, trimming them with a golden line while the plains below were still in darkness.

Abi woke, drowsy until the shock of remembering made her tangle in her sleeping bag as she struggled to get out.

"Grandad!" she cried out.

"Steady, Abi," he said in a voice that was not much more than a whisper. "I'm still here. I could do with some warming, and some more tablets, though."

Abi got the sleeping bag off her legs, and spread it gently over Grandad's blankets.

"I'll make up the fire and get you coffee," she said.

They heard the sound of the helicopter from the east a few minutes after they had finished breakfast. Abi got two flares and ran down to the widest clearing. Without the mountains to block the signal, she knew the CB would work from the valley floor to anyone in the sky. Abi switched it on.

"Westward Ho to helicopter. Westward Ho to helicopter," she called.

"Is that you, Abi?" Margot answered.

"Mum!" Abi cried. "Where are you?"

"In the helicopter," Margot said.

Abi burst into tears.

"Fire a distress flare, Abi," Margot said softly.

Abi found a flare and set it off. It went high into the sky, trailing orange smoke, then curved over and fell.

"We can see it!" Margot called. "We're nearly there."

A few moments later the helicopter came sweeping over the ridge, tilted slightly, slid across the sky, and came slowly down.

Mum and a man carrying a medical case climbed out. They ducked their heads and ran across to Abi.

"Oh, Abi!" Margot cried, giving her a

quick hug. "Where's Grandad?"

Abi pointed and ran. Margot and the man followed, dropping to their knees when they reached Grandad. He reached out and took Margot's hand and gave it a brief kiss.

But Margot didn't notice. Her horrified eyes were on the dead lion.

"I'm Paul," the man said. He put a stethoscope to Grandad's chest with one hand, and took Grandad's wrist in the other to check his pulse. "I'm a doctor. You don't look too bad, sir."

Paul looked at Grandad's leg. "That's some splint!" he said admiringly. "I don't think we'll take that off till you're in hospital!" He turned to Margot. "Will you go back and tell Flavio we'll need the stretcher, please?"

In fifteen minutes, they had Grandad on a stretcher locked to the side of the helicopter. Flavio was back at the controls. Paul turned to Abi and Margot.

"It might take some time to get him back on his feet," he shouted through the sound of the engine and blades. "But it's not going to slow him down too much. Tough people for a tough life, eh?"

Paul gave them a quick grin, and

The helicopter's ability to fly slowly and to hover make it ideal for search and rescue operations.

climbed aboard. The swishing blades picked up speed, and lifted the helicopter away.

It was only then Abi realised Margot had come to stay.

"I'm going to share half your adventure," Margot said. "And Dad's coming up on the bike in a few days to share the last. But, that lion...?"

"It's been following us," Abi said. "We didn't want to worry you."

Margot took a deep breath, and held it for several moments. When she spoke, her voice was controlled, but her eyes looked wild.

"I want to see what Abe Covey wanted to see," she said.

"It wasn't dangerous," Abi said. "Not till last night."

"Just show me the top of the mountain," Margot said.

They climbed together until they stood on the ridge. They gazed over the plains to the distant horizon. "I wonder what's over that horizon?" Abi said. "One day I'm going to go and see."

Where to from here?

If you would like to know more about adventures, you are very lucky, because book libraries, video libraries and the Internet have a golden harvest of adventure just waiting for you to gather.

You can begin with short versions of popular books like *Robinson Crusoe* and continue through myriad titles that take you on travels through outer space.

Some stories are fictional, some fact, and some are fiction exploring what may or will be fact in the future.

And try the Internet for adventures of the past as well as adventures that are happening right now. Many or our modern adventurers keep the world in touch with their adventures on web pages, with photographs included.

Type: "adventure" into a search engine such as google.com. You'll be amazed at what some people, including young children, are doing right now.

And don't forget to read the companion volume in Phenomena, *Awesome Adventures*.

Roger's note

I've ridden horses; I've climbed (very small) mountains, and I've slept under the stars...but I've never gone on an adventure such as Abi had in following the dreams of old Abe Covey.

I wish I had. Maybe I should have followed some of the cattle trails my father used moving the big mobs across Australia's harsh inland country. Or the route he took leading an Australian–American oil search across the centre of Australia to its western shores.

Or perhaps I should be content with writing down the dreams of what I wish I had done so that people like you can read them and be inspired to go out and do something special yourselves?

I think I will settle for that.

I hope some of you who read my

fictional adventures will be inspired to plan adventures for yourselves. Don't hurry. It's best to plan them years ahead. Something that really interests you. Something worth doing.